# Vision Board Success

*How To Get Everything You Want With Vision Boards!*

# Vision Board Success

## *How To Get Everything You Want With Vision Boards!*

### S. F. Howe

Diamond Star Press
Los Angeles

**Vision Board Success**: How To Get Everything You Want With Vision Boards!

Copyright © 2018 S. F. Howe
Published by Diamond Star Press

Second Edition
Trade Paperback
ISBN 13: 978-1-7324591-1-3
ISBN 10: 1-73245-911-8

All rights reserved. No part of this book may be reproduced in any form or by any electronic or mechanical means, including information storage and retrieval systems, without written permission from the author, except in the case of a reviewer, who may quote brief passages in a review. Please direct all inquiries to info@diamondstarpress.com.

Any trademarks, service marks, product names or company names cited herein are assumed to be the property of their respective owners, and are used only for reference. There is no implied endorsement if we use one of these terms.

Disclaimer and Terms of Use: No information contained in this book should be considered as physical, health related, financial, tax, or legal advice. Your reliance upon information and content obtained by you at or through this publication is solely at your own risk. The author assumes no liability or responsibility for damage or injury to you, other persons, or property arising from any use of any product, information, idea, or instruction contained in the content provided to you through this book. Furthermore, the fact that an organization, book or website is referred to in this work as a citation and/or a potential source of further information does not mean that the Author or the Publisher endorses the information the organization, book or website may provide or recommendations it may make. Readers should also be aware that internet websites listed in this work may have changed or disappeared between when this work was written and when it is read.

# Books by S. F. Howe

### Matrix Man
How To Become Enlightened, Happy And Free In An Illusion World

### The Top Ten Myths Of Enlightenment
Exposing The Truth About Spiritual Enlightenment That Will Set You Free!

### The Bringer
Waking Up To The Mind Control Programs Of The Matrix Reality
*Coming Soon!*

### Secrets Of The Plant Whisperer
How To Care For, Connect, And Communicate With Your House Plants

### Your Plant Speaks!
How To Use Your Houseplant As A Therapist
*Coming Soon!*

### Vision Board Success
How To Get Everything You Want With Vision Boards!

### Sex Yoga
The 7 Easy Steps To A Mind-Blowing Kundalini Awakening!

**Morning Routine For Night Owls**
How To Supercharge Your Day With A Gentle Yet Powerful Morning Routine!

**Transgender America**
Spirit, Identity, And The Emergence Of The Third Gender

**When Nothing Else Works**
How To Cure Your Lower Back Pain Fast!

# Bonus Gift

As my thanks to you for reading *Vision Board Success: How to Get Everything You Want With Vision Boards!* I would like you to have a free starter library of two bonus ebooks, "The Law of Attraction" and "The Secrets of Success." The information and techniques offered in these ebooks perfectly complement *Vision Board Success.* They will increase your understanding of how to use the power of Vision Boards to achieve your goals, and accelerate your progress toward creating an ideal and fulfilling life.

To receive your free gift, just send an email to info@diamondstarpress.com with proof of purchase and "Send Vision Board Gift" in the subject field, and we will get your bonus ebooks out to you right away. Do it now before you forget!

# Table of Contents

| | |
|---|---:|
| Author Preface | 1 |
| Introducing Vision Board Success | 3 |
| Chapter One<br>*The Power of Visualization* | 7 |
| Chapter Two<br>*The Three Scientific Laws of Vision Board Success* | 19 |
| Chapter Three<br>*The 8 Essential Materials for Constructing a Vision Board* | 23 |
| Chapter Four<br>*Avoiding the Five Common Pitfalls* | 25 |
| Chapter Five<br>*The Four Rules of Proper Goal-Setting* | 29 |
| Chapter Six<br>*Making Your Vision Board in Four Easy Steps* | 33 |
| Chapter Seven<br>*Using the Vision Board* | 37 |
| Chapter Eight<br>*The Centering Meditation* | 41 |
| Chapter Nine<br>*Healing the Subconscious* | 47 |
| Chapter Ten<br>*The Balance Factor* | 55 |
| Chapter Eleven<br>*Your Inner Genie* | 61 |

| | |
|---|---|
| Chapter Twelve<br>*Daily Program for Success* | 65 |
| Did You Enjoy This Book? | 75 |
| Books by S. F. Howe | 77 |
| About the Author | 81 |
| Bonus Gift | 83 |

# Author Preface

Welcome to **Vision Board Success**! You have just taken your first step toward making all your dreams come true using the success power of vision boards. In this book you will learn everything you need to know to make a vision board that will transform your dreams into reality. Best of all, the process is simple and straightforward, and lots of fun! Just decide what it is you want, follow the easy steps to assembling your vision board, meditate on it daily, and you will start to see magic happen in your life.

Inside these pages, prepare to discover:

* What a vision board is and why it is your pathway to personal fulfillment

* How to use the vision board to turn yourself into a success magnet

# VISION BOARD SUCCESS

\* What three scientific laws you must fully understand in order to activate your vision board success

\*Why the vision board is so powerful, you need to be very careful what you wish for

\*How to optimize your vision board to maximize the power and speed with which it delivers results

…and much, much more.

It is my pleasure to introduce you to this magical method for getting everything you want in life. So hold onto your hat and get ready, get set, go!

# Introducing Vision Board Success

Congratulations! You have just embarked on an exciting journey to success and fulfillment. All you need to do is read this material and follow the step-by-step instructions. But first, a few questions and answers in order to help you understand how this amazing method works.

**What is a Vision Board?**

A vision board is a concrete visual picture of your having and experiencing something you truly desire. This is accomplished by gathering together pictures, symbols, words and photos related to your goal and attaching them to a surface, such as a piece of poster board. The resulting visual collage shows you having and experiencing your goal right now. It is a lasting visual image of success in achieving your goal which you can view as often as you like to inspire you toward your goal and to keep it fixed clearly in your mind.

But that's not all –

## How does the Vision Board work and why is it so powerful?

There is a little-known secret of success found in the occult power of visualization, and a vision board is one of the most powerful methods of visualization known to man. 'Visualization' means to form a picture of something in your mind which is not in sight. It is important to know that human beings think in pictures – not in thoughts, words, or feelings – but in pictures within the mind. To prove this for yourself, try to think of something without seeing a picture of whatever you are thinking of flash through your mind. You will find that this is impossible.

Anything you do, whether it is getting up for a glass of water, painting a canvas, or achieving

## Introducing Vision Board Success

an Olympic medal starts as a mental picture. If you reflect on your life, you will see that this is true. By keeping a clear picture in your mind of your goal you can achieve anything you desire.

The vision board works so effectively because it helps you establish and sustain this clear picture of your objective by concentrating and focusing your mental and psychic energies,. Think of it – any desire you have for love, health, wealth, success, beauty, friendship, or a particular material goal, such as a new car or a vacation, can be realized if you truly want it and follow the rules to creating a successful vision board that I provide in this book!

In the chapters that follow you will learn the three scientific laws of vision board success that you must understand to maximize your own success. Then I will show you how to assemble everything you need to make a powerful vision board, and I will alert you to the common pitfalls in the use of vision boards that can hinder your success. Next I will help you choose your goal correctly so as to increase its likelihood of realization, and then I will take you through the whole construction process start to finish. This book continues with a few words about creating vision boards with others and the all-important how-to instructions for using your vision board correctly to rapidly manifest your desires.

This expanded second edition also contains invaluable information on meditation, manifesting techniques and how to maintain the success mindset and lifestyle. The combination of the vision board training with this new information will skyrocket your ability to dramatically change your life.

Are you ready? Let us begin.

*Chapter One*

# The Power of Visualization

Do you secretly believe vision boards should have a disclaimer in small print underneath them like your newspaper astrology column does: for entertainment only? Or perhaps you see vision boards as a kind of woo woo, new age technique that relies solely on faith and hope. On the other hand, maybe you imagine it works like the placebo effect, the way sugar pills do in medical studies. If so, you will be happy to discover that science has researched visualization and supports the power of visualization and the use of a vision board for manifesting goals.

Because a vision board is highly interactive during the construction phase, as well as visually stimulating and emotionally engaging, it ranks as one of the most effective of the many visualization techniques, and, undoubtedly, the most fun! To give you utmost confidence in the value of creating your first vision board, this chapter presents an overview of different methods of visualization and then delves into some of the fascinating scientific research findings on visualization techniques. You will discover how effective vision boards and other simple visualization exercises are in helping you achieve your dreams.

**Visualization Techniques**

There are a variety of approaches you can take to harness the power of visualization. When it comes to vision boards, you probably know that they involve choosing a goal and compiling images into a collage that signifies achieving that goal. But did you also know that while you are using sensory cues to construct the vision board,

## The Power of Visualization

your brain is doing important subconscious work that will help you bring this imagined reality into being?

That process is further aided by another powerful visualization technique, visualization meditation, which is the practice of focusing on a particular image or symbol, whether externally, such as your vision board hanging on the wall, or internally, such as an imagined scene. These two techniques, vision boards and visualization meditation combine to create the secret recipe behind the power of vision boards, and will be discussed further in later chapters.

However, there are other important visualization techniques worthy of consideration, such as receptive visualization which involves directing a movie of what you want to happen in your head. While imagining the scene in vivid detail, you attempt to stimulate every one of your senses, visualizing the colors, smells, sounds, and sensations in order to make it feel as real as possible.

# VISION BOARD SUCCESS

Altered memory visualization is like receptive visualization, except that you look backwards at a negative experience and re-imagine a better outcome. A key part of all visualization techniques is being able to arouse strong emotions that duplicate how you would actually feel if you achieved your goal and it is part of your life at this very moment.

**Brain Imagery Research**

For the purposes of scientific study, visualization is defined as mental imagery used to help manifest a goal or desire. Surprisingly, imagery can replicate the same patterns in the brain as actually experiencing something with the physical senses.

In a 2005 paper by Helder Bertolo, a Portuguese professor at the School of Medicine of the University of Lisbon, 10 patients who had been blind from birth participated in tests that measured the electrical activity of their brains while being woken up periodically from sleep to recall their dreams. These tests were compared to those of 9 sighted persons undergoing the same procedure, and the results were found to be similar. Even though the blind participants had never experienced the act of "seeing," they were able to reproduce visual experiences in their brains and even draw the contents of their dreams.

This indicates that mental imagery may give you the opportunity to experience events without having to perceive the event with your physical senses.

As if this is not enough evidence that mental imagery can replicate physical experiences, another study from 2007 tested athletes who practiced an exercise in their minds against participants who did the exercise with their bodies. Professors Shackell and Standing of Bishop's University concluded that the group using mental training had the most gains.

## Achieving Goals

Whatever type of visualization technique you use, research shows that visualization effectively helps you reach your goals. First, mental imagery enhances the ability to implement intentions. A team of professors in Montreal, Canada, tested the theory that intention combined with mental imagery would increase the likelihood that a group of students would carry out their intention. 48 students at a large North American University were invited to participate in the study and were given a mundane task to complete. The students were divided randomly into two groups: one group simply wrote out how they would complete the task and the other group wrote out their implementation plan *and* were asked to close their eyes and imagine how they would complete the task (applying receptive visualization). 88% of the students who employed the visualization completed the task compared to only 60% of the students who only wrote out the task.

Do you want to eat more fruit? Visualization can help you achieve that goal, too. In 2009, some of the same scientists from the task completion study mentioned above were interested in seeing if visualization would apply in an area where most of us would like to do better: eating healthier foods. This time, the researchers sought volunteers from among the students going to the cafeteria of the North American University. Again, where the students paired their intention to eat more fruit with receptive visualization of that activity, the students consumed more fruit.

**Athletic Performance**

Visualization also concretely enhances physical performance. In a study using receptive visualization techniques, researchers at Sacred Heart University in Milan, Italy, studied the performance of 60 female university students. These students were divided into random groups that either practiced basketball lay-ups physically, or combined the physical practice with mental imagery. The group that used mental imagery showed better coordination and accuracy in their performance.

## Health

Visualization may impact disease symptoms, too. In a famous article by Dr. O. Carl Simonton and two other researchers, Dr. Simonton found that visualization could aid cancer patients in surviving longer than patients who did not practice visualization. Dr. Simonton employed techniques such as relaxation exercises, guided imagery (a form of receptive visualization where the participant is led through the visualization process by another person) and meditation to bring the patient to a more positive outcome.

## Happiness

What if your goals are more abstract – like just being happier? In a 1997 study of 28 healthy adults, researchers examined whether guided imagery and music therapy could positively affect mood and cortisol levels. Unlike the controls, the participants who received the guided imagery and music therapy exhibited less depression and a decrease in cortisol.

# The Power of Visualization

Another study concluded that where participants had higher levels of mental imagery ability, they enjoyed a greater degree of well-being. Australian professors Odou and Vella-Brodrick looked at 210 adult participants, focusing on measuring their well-being and their mental imagery ability (the vividness of the mental images and the ability of the individual to control the images). The adults with the highest mental imagery abilities experienced greater levels of happiness.

In conclusion, whatever visualization technique you choose, you can realize concrete benefits from employing these techniques. Whether you want to eat more fruit, be happier or achieve your biggest ambitions, visualization is one of the best ways to help you reach that goal. The next chapter begins your training in creating vision boards. It teaches you how to establish and maintain the correct mindset as the foundation for your vision board success.

## Sources

Alfonso, J., Caracual, A., Delgado-Pastor, L., & Verdejo-Garcia, A. (2011). Combined goal management training and mindfulness meditation improve execution functions and decision-making performance in abstinent polysubstance abusers. *Drug and Alcohol Dependence*, 117(2011).

Bertolo, H., (2005). Visual imagery without visual perception? *Psicologica*, 26.

Gagiolo, A., Morganti, L., Mondoni, M., & Antonietti, A., (2013). Benefits of Combined Mental and Physical Training in Learning Complex Motor Skill in Basketball. *Psychology*, 4(9A2). http://dx.doi.org/10.4236/psych.2013.49A2001

Knauper, B., McCollam, A., Rosen-Brown, A., Lacaille, E., & Roseman, M. (2009). Fruitful plans: Adding targeted mental imagery to implementation increases fruit consumption. *Psychology and Health*, 26(5).

Knauper, B., Roseman, M., Johnson, P., & Krantz., L. (2009). Using Mental Imagery to Enhance the Effectiveness of Implementation Intentions. *Current Psychology*, 28. DOI 10.1007/s12144-009-9055-0

McKinney, C., Antoni, M., Kumar, M., TIms., F., & McCabe, P. (1997). Effects of guided imagery and music (GIM) therapy on mood and cortisol in healthy adults. *Health Psychology*, 16(4).

Odou, N., & Vella-Brodrick, D. (2011). The Efficacy of Positive Psychology Interventions to Increase Well-Being and the Role of Mental Imagery Ability. *Social Indicators Research*, (2013). DOI 10.1007/s11205-011-9919-1

Shackell, E., & Standing, L., (2007). Mind Over Matter: Mental Training Increases Physical

Strength. *North American Journal of Psychology*, 9(1).

Simonton, O., Matthews-Simonton, S., & Sparks, T. (1980). Psychological intervention in the treatment of cancer. *Psychosomatics*, 21(3). https://doi.org/10.1016/S0033-3182(80)73697-6/

*Chapter Two*

# The Three Scientific Laws of Vision Board Success

It is important to understand the three scientific laws of vision board success in order to take maximum advantage of the opportunity that is presented in this book. Go over these laws slowly and with full attention. Ponder the meaning of them. Your success depends upon it!

**Law #1: You Create Your Reality According To Your Beliefs About What Is Possible For You.**

This means that by your habitual thoughts, attitudes and beliefs, you set the boundaries within which the daily drama of your life unfolds. You get what you see yourself as capable of getting, and that which seems to elude your grasp becomes the thing you dream about, wondering if it will ever come true.

This kind of limited thinking, like a child pressing his nose against a candy store window, will never achieve success. People who are successful always believe that they can get what they want. They have confidence in their abilities and naturally visualize themselves having what they want before they go after it.

If you do not have the positive belief that you truly can have what you want, then the life you experience will have all kinds of problems, limitations and lack. You will never have enough money, love, material goods, opportunity, health, etc.

Fortunately, you can change your experience by changing your belief in what is possible for you. Your life is not a fixed thing! It is vital and flexible and can be transformed by your thoughts. Positive thoughts and images create positive results.

## Law #2: There Are No Limitations On What You Can Have In Life.

The truth is, the universe you inhabit is a place of unlimited abundance and good, and anything you want is waiting to be claimed by you through your positive thoughts and visualizations. You, as an integral part of the universe, just by virtue of being here, are entitled to have anything you want as long as it harms no one else. And you will get it if you really want it and go about the proper way of getting it.

Most people do not believe the principle just stated. They think that there is not enough to go around. They are limited by the belief in scarcity. For example, many people think that there is only so much money in the world, that only a limited amount of food is available, or that only a select or lucky few can be successful. Do you think this way? Do you hold the belief in scarcity?

Remember –

**Law #3: You Deserve And Are Entitled To Get Whatever You Want In Life.**

Many people believe that they do not deserve to get what they truly want. Some people think they are not good enough or worthy enough to get what they want, whether it is a brand new luxury car, a vacation in Hawaii, good health, or a loving relationship. Perhaps they did something wrong in the past for which they have not forgiven themselves. Perhaps they have a low opinion of themselves. Maybe they think they will have bad luck all of their lives.

Do you think or believe this way? Remember, you are an inseparable part of the Universe. As such, you deserve and are entitled to have your desires fulfilled, and there is nothing that is too good to be true.

## Chapter Three

# The Eight Essential Materials for Constructing a Vision Board

You already have the two most important elements for success with your vision board: your desire to achieve a certain goal and your willingness to learn how to create and use a vision board to help you achieve that goal.

In addition to those critical elements, you will need time – not a great deal, but enough to plan out, construct and reflect upon your vision board in a calm, unhurried and meaningful manner.

Lastly, you will need the following materials:

# VISION BOARD SUCCESS

* Writing paper
* Writing tools: pen, pencil, magic markers, etc. (Stick-on letters and stencils can be purchased in art and stationery stores.)
* Scissors
* Glue, paste or scotch tape
* A sturdy surface (preferably poster board, but paper, wood, fiberboard, corkboard, part of a wall, etc., can be used)
* Books, magazines, newspapers, internet – any kind of source from which you may find pictures and/or words to cut out or print out. You can also make your own drawings or combine them with the pictures.
* Photographs of yourself (and anyone else that is participating if there is a common goal) which you will need to place upon your vision board. Color images are preferable.
* Be creative. You may attach to your surface anything that brings your goal alive for you.

*Chapter Four*

# Avoiding the Five Common Pitfalls

In the following chapter I will discuss how to set your goals for maximum success. But first, dear reader, some warnings are in order to protect you from the misuse of this technique.

**First** – Because you <u>will</u> get what you want, be quite careful about what you ask for. The best way to illustrate this warning is to have you reflect back upon your life and look at the things you wanted that you later regretted receiving. We have all had one or more of these experiences in life.

## VISION BOARD SUCCESS

Perhaps you manifested a beautiful, high end sports car which turned out to be temperamental, expensive to keep up and repair, required sky-high insurance premiums and was stolen once a year. Or maybe you couldn't live without a relationship with that certain someone who later revealed him or herself to be psychologically and temperamentally unsuitable for you.

Therefore, I am urging you to do the best you can to ensure that what you want will be good for you in the long run.

**Second** – Never make a vision board for the purpose of causing harm to others. By doing so, you set up the conditions for harm to come to you! Trust me on this.

**Third** – If you have a health problem, be sure to get proper medical attention. Then use your vision board as an aid to speed your recovery.

**Fourth** – Do not be anxious about achieving your goal. A relaxed but focused attitude is the key to success.

**Fifth** – Now that you are about to begin the process of using a vision board for success, do

## Avoiding the Five Common Pitfalls

not tell anybody what you are doing. Of course, if you are making a vision board along with another person or persons in order to reach a common goal, you will not keep it a secret from them. But as for others, even good friends, do keep it from them until you get what you want. One reason for this is that you don't want to give others the opportunity to negate what you are doing. And more importantly, by telling others, you scatter and weaken the concentration of powerful psychic energy needed to achieve results.

*Chapter Five*

# The Four Rules of Proper Goal-Setting

Before you create your vision board you must decide what goal you wish to focus on. I highly recommend focusing your first vision board on one goal. The one goal at a time rule more often than not leads to a breakthrough in manifesting an important goal and can become your primary technique for bringing your most cherished desires into your reality. On the other hand, once you have become familiar with the process and the vision board has proven itself to you, you can try

# VISION BOARD SUCCESS

constructing large and colorful boards for multiple goals.

**I. Identify Your Goal**

Go to a place where you can be alone and undisturbed and, if you have not already done so, decide exactly what goal you want to focus on and write it down. Be specific. It is not enough, for example, to merely want a new job. Specify for yourself, and then write down, the type of job you want, including vital aspects such as salary, position, approximate date you start work, work environment, dress code, personality characteristics of fellow employees, possibilities for advancement, range of personal freedom, etc. – anything that is important to you in a job. Then write down a statement which indicates you have already attained your goal, such as, "I, Joe, am the Personnel Manager at Smith Company and I am enjoying the challenges and rewards of my new, highly paid job.

The Four Rules of Proper Goal-Setting

## II. Reflect On Your Goal

After you have written down exactly what you want along with your statement about actually having it, ask yourself: Is this what I really want? Can I be more specific? Have I left anything out? How will this goal affect my life? How will this goal affect other people in my life? Is this goal something I can really handle? Revise your goal, if necessary, until you are clear about what you want and feel certain it will be a positive change in your life.

## III. Finalize Your Goal

Make a final copy of your goal after all revisions are made. You will place this on your vision board. It is also helpful to make additional copies (perhaps on cards or smaller pieces of paper) which you may carry with you or place in spots where you can see them daily. This will further intensify and focus your energies around your goal.

Don't hesitate to make changes to your goal as time passes. It's a natural process to have new ideas or desires related to your goal surface over time. If they do, just rewrite your goal and follow the above steps, replacing the old version with the new.

**IV. You Have It Now**

Always state your goal in the present, as if it has already manifested and is in your life now. Never phrase your goal as if it is a future event. The proper attitude to take is that you have your goal <u>now</u>. This frame of mind reinforces your power to create and have what you want in the present moment and is essential to your success. Remember, if you phrase the goal in the future, such as "I will have xyz job," you are instructing your creative power to always keep the goal in the future and never bring it into your present reality. Set goals the smart way by seeing them as having already happened.

*Chapter Six*

# Making Your Vision Board in Four Easy Steps

**S****tep One**: Take out the magazines and other materials you have collected. Calmly flip through your materials, keeping an eye out for pictures, photographs, pictorial advertisements and/or headlines that represent what you want. For example, if you want a trip to Hawaii, you might select pictures containing scenes with beaches, palm trees, people sipping tropical drinks, surfers, sugar, pineapple or coffee plantations, people dressed in vacation attire, a couple walking along a beach, a tropical sunset, people on a ship or boat, activities such as fishing, swimming, strolling, eating, shopping, etc. Your goal of a trip to Hawaii may mean more to you, such as a place to reflect or meditate, a place of healing, discovery or new adventure. Find pictures and any other items which will represent these experiences to you.

**Step Two**: Cut out the pictures, assemble your items and arrange them on your poster board or any other surface you have selected for your vision board. Evaluate your selections to make sure you have a complete visual representation of your goal. Add, subtract, or rearrange your materials so that the resulting image is complete and aesthetically pleasing. Paste or otherwise secure them onto the surface. Don't forget to place photos of yourself anywhere you like on the vision board. Wherever there is a face of someone in a picture that might represent you, paste your face over it. If religion is an important part of your life, add a symbol of your faith to the vision board, such as

## Making Your Vision Board in Four Easy Steps

a picture of Jesus or any personal religious image.

**Step Three**: Affirmations, which are positive statements about your goal, should be included on your vision board. For example, if your objective is a loving relationship your affirmation might be: "Here I am enjoying a full life with my perfect mate." You can also take crayons or markers and write key words in large letters, such as FUN, ADVENTURE, SUCCESS, LOVE, HEALTH, which fit into the scheme of what you want to get. It is always wise to include the Master Affirmation, "I now receive this or something better in the best possible way for me."

**Step Four**: For best results use lots of color on your vision board. Be creative. Use your imagination. Enjoy yourself.

**Step Five** (Optional): If your goal includes the presence of others for its accomplishment, it is fun and helpful to make your vision board together. Not only is a vision board for a family goal an enjoyable way to bring your family

# VISION BOARD SUCCESS

together for one or more pleasurable evenings, but this shared focus will speed your goal into realization. Don't forget to include everyone's picture on the vision board!

*Chapter Seven*

# Using the Vision Board

When you have finished your vision board to your satisfaction, pat yourself on the back for a job well done and then select a place to put up the vision board. It should be a location, such as a bedroom wall, where you will easily see it at least several times a day.

Make a point to spend a few minutes every day meditating on your vision board. The more time you spend the better, but aim for at least twice per day, morning and evening, for approximately five to ten minutes each time. When you look at your vision board, don't try to figure out how your desire will come about – it's important that you don't think about the 'how.' Just look at the pictures, see yourself in them. Actively imagine that you are there and have already gotten what you want. Feel the joy and satisfaction you would feel if it were already so.

That's it! With regular meditation on your vision board, it will quickly start working for you. Soon you will achieve your goal. All you have to do is keep your eyes and ears open for the opportunities that are sure to come along which will enable you to have what you want. When these opportunities appear, take action on them immediately and you will soon be living the life of your dreams.

This chapter concludes your preparation and training for successfully creating and using vision boards and is complete unto itself. However, the next five chapters are for those of you who wish to go deeper into the workings of your subconscious mind, exploring the role beliefs play in reality creation, and how to best use your subconscious mind to help manifest

## Using the Vision Board

your desires. We also offer a powerful centering technique to help quiet your mind as well as additional tips and tricks to assist in maintaining a positive mindset.

*Chapter Eight*

# The Centering Meditation

To manifest desires consistently, it is important to understand the subconscious mind and how it works to either help or hinder you in achieving your goals. We will begin with a short history of the subconscious within the field of psychology and how certain ingrained beliefs have affected your relationship to your own mind. Then we will guide you through a centering meditation designed to help you quiet your mind and focus within. Using this centering technique before meditating on your vision board will assist the process of making your vision board dreams come true.

In traditional psychology, the subconscious, also known as the unconscious, is believed to be a mental storage site – a repository of memories, emotions, habits and associations. These stored elements form beliefs that operate outside of your awareness, determining who you are, how you act and what your life looks like. To gain control of the undesirable aspects of your life, you must become aware of the elements that are stored in your subconscious and the beliefs they have engendered.

However, in traditional psychology, the subconscious is also portrayed as the saboteur within – something dangerous, something manipulating you, which you shouldn't examine too closely or you might go mad. This causes people to fear their own inner selves and gives rise to the analyst's couch, a safe environment where the subconscious mind can be peeled back layer by layer, like an onion.

## The Centering Meditation

Traditional views of the subconscious die hard. Psychiatry and psychology still tend to demonize the subconscious or marginalize it as an inferior part of mind. Meanwhile the conscious mind is touted as the be all and end all; higher consciousness is denied altogether.

But a deeper understanding of reality reveals that mind is no thing and there are no divisions. Conscious, subconscious, superconscious are not parts of the brain, they are merely descriptive terms applied to the invisible – yet they are terms that have been repeated so often, for so long, in so many ways and places, they are taken as physical fact.

Accessing the power of your subconscious mind begins by letting go of your preconceptions and allowing yourself to move into what I call vertical awareness which is the consciousness of self in the moment. Your thoughts have created a horizontal field of energy stretching in all directions – the literal meaning of feeling scattered or spread too thin. But thought stops in a state of vertical awareness.

# VISION BOARD SUCCESS

The following exercise will give you a glimpse of vertical awareness. Read through the paragraph below, then find a quiet place. Empty your mind of all you were told or thought you knew about the subconscious and enjoy the short meditation that follows. We recommend that you perform this exercise every day before viewing your vision board.

## Centering Meditation

Take a seat in front of your vision board. Close your eyes. Breathe in through your nose to the count of 7. Hold for a few moments. Then breathe out to the count of 8 through partially closed lips. Repeat two more times.

Visualize a net of energy extending horizontally in all directions. This is your thought field. Take a leap of faith and let go of your thought field, trusting that you don't need to hold onto it. Let go of the field and you instantly come back to yourself.

Inner silence signals the arrival of your power. Now imagine your physical body

## The Centering Meditation

enveloped by a column of energy that begins below your feet and extends above your head. In vertical awareness what is above merges with what is below; as above so below.

You feel the rush of unified consciousness and have taken the first step toward unleashing the power of your subconscious mind. You may open your eyes and begin your daily visualization meditation on your vision board.

*Chapter Nine*

# Healing the Subconscious

To develop the power of your subconscious mind, you must free yourself from beliefs that do not serve you. How do you know which beliefs are not working? Look at your life and note everything that you wish were different. Now understand that both these unwanted manifestations and your resistance to them are determined by your beliefs. Subconscious healing begins with clearing the beliefs that attracted the manifestations you wish to change or eliminate.

First, you need to identify the belief. Let us take an example. If you are desiring a new relationship, a true partner in life, but you're alone and single and have been for a very long time, begin with the assumption that a negative subconscious belief about relationships is working against your conscious desire to have a good relationship.

How do you identify that belief? The truth is, there are many beliefs that may be affecting your life. It's best to assume that not just one belief but an entire flotilla, e.g., dozens perhaps even hundreds of beliefs are blocking your desired good.

It would be counterproductive to try to identify and clear each and every belief, as they are not only formed in your subconscious from birth onwards in response to events in your life, but they are also floating around in the mass consciousness, otherwise known as the collective unconscious, and affecting you subconsciously. Your solution is subconscious healing and it begins with raising your awareness of how your desires are impacted by your subconscious beliefs.

## Healing the Subconscious

Here is what you do: Get a pen and two large pieces of paper and find a quiet spot where you will not be disturbed for 30 minutes. Draw a tree on one piece of paper. Don't worry about how it looks; any type of tree, any level of drawing ability will work for the purposes of this exercise. Now draw branches on the tree and make 30-50 circles on the branches to represent leaves. Inside of each circle, write down one reason for why you don't have a relationship. If you can't think of at least 30 reasons, just pretend to have reasons. Think of reasons your friends have mentioned, or reasons of characters in movies or books.

Your goal is to write down at least 30 reasons such as 'I'm too fat, "I'm afraid of losing my independence," "I'm afraid of being abandoned," "men cause conflict," "men are demanding," "all the good ones are taken," etc. Now draw one big leaf at the very top of this tree, like the star on a Christmas tree. This leaf will represent the collective unconscious. Label it

"All negative beliefs about relationships since the beginning of time."

Once you have completed your negative beliefs tree, enjoy your handiwork for a moment. Recognize the large number of negative ideas that are affecting your ability to attract the right relationship. But realize also that these are only the ones that you are conscious of. For every conscious negative, there are ten or more unconscious beliefs.

Perhaps you now realize why you don't have this relationship. At this point, you also have the freedom to decide consciously not to have a relationship. It is always your choice. Perhaps you feel compelled to seek something that you don't really want! It's okay to stop seeking and just be where you're at in your life.

But if you truly desire to have a relationship with your right partner, then you must put aside the negative beliefs tree and draw another tree, the positive beliefs tree. On the branches of this tree, fill 30-50 circles with good reasons for having a relationship. When you are done, put a big circle on top of that tree to represent the collective unconscious and write "All positive relationship beliefs since the beginning of time."

Place the two trees side by side. Now you see clearly in front of you how you are split, how there is a duality within, one side pulling you in a negative direction, the other pulling you in a positive direction. This duality is what must be healed. Those who succeed in achieving their desires are integrated at the subconscious level. Subconscious healing occurs when you achieve this integration. Your desired good then outpictures in your reality in a natural and organic way or may be quickly manifested by using vision boards and other visualization techniques.

One way of releasing subconscious beliefs that don't serve you is to take each belief one by one and ask yourself, "Can I let go of this?" Sense within for a 'yes' answer. The goal is to reach a 'yes' as quickly as possible. When you get a 'yes,' then ask yourself, "Can I let go of this right now?" Again seek within for a 'yes.' When you answer 'yes,' then ask, "How would it feel to not have this belief?" Sense the joy and lightness within.

If you go through this process with each negative belief after drawing the positive and negative trees, you will subtly shift the energetic balance of negative and positive beliefs toward the positives you have listed, and as a result are far more likely to attract the mate you desire. The good news is that this shift in balance does not require discovering and clearing every single negative belief that might be floating around in your subconscious. By applying it to the beliefs listed on your negative beliefs tree, it will effect enough change toward the positive to make a difference.

This technique can speed up the manifestation of any unfulfilled desire. Therefore, be sure to practice this technique with your vision board goals. We recommend using it ahead of time to clear the path for a speedier result. On the other hand, you may apply it later on if results are delayed or if you find yourself

## Healing the Subconscious

resisting meditating on the vision board or taking action on your goal. Either way, use this technique and look for an exciting breakthrough!

## Chapter Ten

# The Balance Factor

To paraphrase the great Russian philosopher, G. I. Gurdjieff, "The mind is like a drunken monkey, lurching from thought to thought throughout your waking hours." Perhaps you can recognize the truth of this by observing the constant activity of your own mind and by also noting the inconsistencies in what other people say or do. What this means for you is that in order to achieve vision board goals and fulfill dreams you need to be single-minded, which begins with quieting the incessant activity of your mind. Your mind automatically becomes quieter when you let go of the thought grid — your energy field of habitual thoughts and thought patterns — and focus in the present moment, in what I call vertical awareness.

Your emotions are like the ocean, sometimes calm, sometimes stormy. You react to your thoughts emotionally according to your conditioning and you are also conditioned to believe your thoughts. Imagine the freedom in recognizing that your thoughts don't have to be taken seriously. That's a completely new idea, isn't it? You will always have thoughts, but you don't have to believe what they are telling you; in other words, you don't have to give your thoughts power.

In our culture, we've been taught that what we think is not only important, it is correct, and so we take our thoughts quite seriously. But the reality is that the activity of thought is like the activity of fish in a sea. If the sea is consciousness then fish are our thoughts, coming and going, continually swimming around. They don't belong to us personally, being largely an expression of the cultural mind. Otherwise known as the collective unconscious, the cultural mind primarily contains age-old beliefs, cultural biases and superstitions.

The thoughts you have throughout the day stir up emotions that cause mood swings in a positive or negative direction. Many of us strive to stay positive, not realizing that the effort to be positive generates a build-up of negative energy. This build-up inevitably results in your mood dipping until your positive state is balanced out with a negative state. Now you know why you are unable to sustain a positive frame of mind for very long. But if you were to allow positive and negative thoughts to move through you without becoming attached to them, you could easily maintain a place of emotional balance.

Only emotional balance brings the equilibrium that enables you to access your personal power. Balance is a higher state of consciousness than either the negative side or the positive side. Those two opposites trigger each other endlessly; one is simply the mirror of the other. Balance is a state of mind that exists in the gap between positive and negative, light and dark. It enables you to observe the events of your everyday life without becoming overly attached to the outcome. It does not ensure the absence of ups and downs, it simply allows you to view events with a degree of objectivity. Another way of expressing the word 'balance' is objective consciousness or non-attachment.

How do you achieve non-attachment in the face of your strong wishes, wants, needs and desires? You achieve it by knowing the truth about how you really manifest. When you understand that manifesting is your higher power's job and that your job is to stay present and follow your motivation and inspiration, you will get busy fulfilling your role.

A higher order of existence opens up when you are present in the moment and emotionally balanced. Your subconscious mind then provides you with the ideas, the energy and the inspiration to pursue certain activities and relationships. When you take note of and follow

## The Balance Factor

this inner guidance, your desires are fulfilled in unexpected ways.

The following chapter presents a simple, playful way to help you maintain this state of balance. If you make a habit of it, it will facilitate the manifesting of your vision board goals.

## Chapter Eleven

# Your Inner Genie

We previously discussed how your thoughts trigger emotional reactions which affect your judgment, your actions and ultimately the outcome of events. We looked at how the effort to 'think positive,' in order to positively affect the outcome of events, can trigger an emotional backlash of suppressed negativity which eventually finds its way to the surface and outpictures as depression or as an undesired event.

The movement from feeling up to feeling down, and vice versa, is an ongoing cycle in most people's lives. It demonstrates how thought can shift your vibrational frequency from the higher range of your bandwidth, where you automatically feel good, to the lower range, where you automatically feel bad.

When you reach a certain point on either end of your bandwidth, you begin to move in the opposite direction. The lower you go, the higher you go, and the cycle is repeated ad infinitum. At the energetic level, what is known as bipolar disorder is simply this yo-yo effect played out on the outermost edges of your bandwidth where your energy is least stable.

I've been experimenting with a fun method that helps you avoid dwelling on negative ideas without triggering an emotional backlash. Envision your subconscious mind as an inner genie with the power to fulfill all of your commands. By virtue of the law of attraction – which teaches that you get what you focus on and what you focus on expands – your inner genie takes everything you say or think literally and fulfills your commands indiscriminately.

## Your Inner Genie

The intent of this exercise is to help you stay in energetic harmony with your vision board goal or any other goals and desires. For example, if your vision board is set up around a weight loss goal, whenever you catch yourself visualizing, speaking, or thinking something negative or undesirable such as, "I'm gaining weight," imagine that your overeager genie snaps his fingers three times and cries, "So be it!" This will jolt you out of your unconscious thinking habit when you realize you have just added energy to an unwanted event.

Next, all you have to say is, "Cancel," and the command is deleted. If you wish, you may then consciously replace it with the thought, "I am slim and healthy," and imagine that the genie snaps his fingers three times and declares, "So be it!"

You'll be surprised at how good this method for managing your thoughts makes you feel. The inner genie technique exposes how often your thoughts or statements unwittingly contribute to a negative outcome, and then quickly restores balance. The end result is a more cheerful mood, which signifies that you are stabilizing at a higher vibration, as well as less negative thoughts and faster and more desirable outcomes. Try it, you'll like it!

*Chapter Twelve*

# Daily Program for Success

Following a daily program for success is the perfect way to accelerate your personal growth and success, not to mention the fulfillment of your vision board goals. Studies have shown that people who are happier tend to be more successful. Science has also proven that a positive mindset results in a happier and more successful life and can be cultivated by employing certain daily practices.

The power of a positive daily routine should not be underestimated in helping you to achieve your goals and dreams. What follows are my recommendations for a program that will put you on the fast track to success and fulfillment.

## MEDITATION

There is no single practice in your self help program that is more important than meditation. Not only is meditation a powerful contributor to health, it is also an invaluable success technique.

Among its dozens of health benefits, meditation has been proven to reduce heart rate, regulate digestion, lower blood pressure, improve quality of sleep and increase immune response. Meditation is also a proven stress reducer that tends to erase worry and anxiety from your mind and helps you think more clearly and effectively.

While you are meditating, your brain waves slow down, which raises your vibrational frequency and aligns you with a higher state of consciousness. From this state of higher awareness, spirituality, creativity and problem-solving are enhanced.

## Daily Program for Success

Now that you know the many ways meditation can help in your quest for personal growth and success, make it the first thing you do each day. Perhaps this is where you combine the centering meditation in Chapter 8 with your vision board visualization meditation. Or, if you prefer to meditate on your vision board at a different time, then you may simply sit in the silence with eyes closed and follow your breathing. Allow your thoughts to pass through your mind without any need to do anything with or about them. If you persist, you will reach an emptying point, where there is total silence. Stay in the silence for as long as is comfortable and allow it to clear and reset your entire being.

## MORNING EXERCISE

The second most important addition to an effective daily program is morning exercise. Exercising in the morning balances and raises your energy and prepares your body for the day ahead. A higher energy level means a higher vibrational frequency which is synonymous with a better day.

An excellent exercise for slow risers is meditative in nature, involving gentle movements and stretching. Some good examples of this are yoga and Tai Chi. But if that's not for you, then do whatever form of exercise you enjoy, whatever raises your energy and spirits and makes you feel good. Science has shown that exercise in any form gives health and mood benefits when performed in the early part of your day.

**WRITE DOWN YOUR GOALS**

A program for success must include a list of your one year goals. Take some quiet time to determine your one year goals and write them down on a piece of paper. You'll keep this paper near your computer or in another location where you will see it frequently.

It is important to write down your goals because it helps keep you focused and on point. Read the list three times per day to impress it upon your subconscious mind. Doing so will support your subconscious mind in bringing relevant opportunities and ideas to your attention. You may update your list or make changes as necessary.

Every day, after your morning meditation and exercise, review your one year list. Then take a few minutes to envision what you desire to experience that day and write down your most important goals for the day. There should be no more than three high priority goals for any given day. These goals should inspire and motivate you.

This combined practice of keeping a one year list and a daily short list helps keep you on track for a year of highly productive days, culminating in the achievement of your most important goals for the year. Needless to say, your vision board can further assist you at every stage in keeping on track with your goals, as will the Inner Genie Technique taught in Chapter 11.

# VISION BOARD SUCCESS

## POSITIVE EXPECTATION

Positive expectation is the engine that keeps you focused, motivated and moving toward your chosen future. Positive expectation is activated by referring frequently to your one year list, making your daily list, taking daily action toward your goals and daily visualizing yourself at the one year point.

Once per day, envision your future self at the one year point and imagine how you will look and feel, what you will do and where you will be on that day when your goals are realized. This powerful practice lifts your spirits and predisposes you to having a sense of positive expectation about the year and your ability to accomplish these goals.

You may later realize that, in your initial enthusiasm, you took on more than you can realistically accomplish in one year. Revising your list periodically to reflect this reassessment is wise. Even if you choose only one major goal, imagine how transformed your life will be if you accomplish that goal in the coming year. Your positive expectation of success greatly increases its likelihood.

## KEEP A JOURNAL

Many successful people love to keep a record of their journey and do so through daily journaling. After your busy day, take a few moments to jot down a few thoughts about the important moments in your day, both good and bad, how you felt about them and how you might handle things differently in the coming day. Don't hesitate to write a prayer to your higher power if you feel the need. The main thing is, the journal is there so that you can express how you really feel. I promise that you will have many amazing healings and revelations in so doing.

Journaling before bedtime sets the stage for healing to take place in your sleep and for new ideas and energy to surface in the new day. So take time to write before you sleep and don't forget to ask for help with what you need.

## LEAD A BALANCED LIFE

All that you are and all that constitutes your life are equally important in your program for success. Ignore any part of the whole at your peril. Because of the holistic nature of reality, you must take a balanced approach to living. Holistic and wholesome are inseparable concepts in that together they constitute a modus operandi for the balanced life. So make sure that your life contains both work and play, that you properly take care of your body, home and property, that you contribute to the well being of others and that you develop your talents and enlighten your spirit.

## SHARE YOUR DISCOVERIES

The fastest way to learn something at a deeper level is to teach it to others. By sharing your success program and your personal development discoveries with others, you strengthen the part of you that is striving to grow and achieve. It's a well-known axiom that whatever you focus on increases. So share your knowledge of personal

## Daily Program for Success

development techniques and get ready for an expansion of your own personal growth.

Thank you for joining me on this journey. You have learned how to make and use vision boards to get everything you want in life and have received additional information to help facilitate the manifestation of your goals. Practice diligently what you have learned and watch your deepest wishes and desires take form before your very eyes.

Before you go, please don't forget to get your free gift, a starter library of two bonus ebooks, "The Law of Attraction" and "The Secrets of Success." The information and techniques offered in those books perfectly complement *Vision Board Success* and will accelerate your progress toward creating an ideal and fulfilling life.

Send an email to info@diamondstarpress.com with "Send Vision Board Gift" in the subject field and proof of purchase, and we will get your free gift out to you right away.

# Did You Enjoy This Book?

Dear Reader,

Thank you for reading this book. I hope you enjoyed *Vision Board Success: How To Get Everything You Want With Vision Boards!*

My main purpose in writing *Vision Board Success* is to empower you to achieve your goals without delay through a fluff-free presentation of the nuts and bolts of using vision boards. This second edition also contains vital information to assist you in maintaining the proper mindset for success.

If you would like to help me reach more readers with this life-changing information, nothing would help more than your writing a brief review on Amazon. It will only take a few seconds, and I would appreciate it very much.

Thanks again, and wishing you the very best!

*S. F. Howe*

# Books by S. F. Howe

## MIND · BODY · SPIRIT

### HIGHER CONSCIOUSNESS

**Matrix Man: How To Become Enlightened, Happy And Free In An Illusion World**

The author reveals a new reality paradigm that will liberate you from the limiting beliefs and programs that prevent a joyful and fulfilling life. Available in print and digital editions.

**The Top Ten Myths Of Enlightenment: Exposing The Truth About Spiritual Enlightenment That Will Set You Free!**

Essential reading for spiritual seekers. What no one else will tell you to help you avoid the pitfalls of the spiritual journey. Available in print and digital editions.

**The Bringer: Waking Up To The Mind Control Programs Of The Matrix Reality**

Available in print and digital editions.
*Coming Soon!*

## PLANT INTELLIGENCE

### Secrets Of The Plant Whisperer: How To Care For, Connect, And Communicate With Your House Plants

A plant whisperer reveals the hidden truth about plants and why relating to them in a conscious way is vital for their health and well-being. Available in print and digital editions.

### Your Plant Speaks!: How To Use Your Houseplant As A Therapist

Let your house plant solve your problems! Discover the little known art of receiving life coaching from your favorite indoor plant.
*Coming Soon!*

## PERSONAL GROWTH

### Vision Board Success: How To Get Everything You Want With Vision Boards!

A powerful technique for achieving your goals and manifesting your desires. Available in print and digital editions.

### Sex Yoga: The 7 Easy Steps To A Mind-Blowing Kundalini Awakening!

A technique for activating the chakras to induce a powerful kundalini experience. Available in print and digital editions.

## Morning Routine For Night Owls: How To Supercharge Your Day With A Gentle Yet Powerful Morning Routine!

Morning rituals aren't only for morning people, and they don't have to be rough and tumble or performed at top speed to set up a perfect day. Welcome to the world of the gentle yet powerful wake-up routine for night owls! Available in print and digital editions.

### CONSCIOUS HEALTH

## Transgender America: Spirit, Identity, And The Emergence Of The Third Gender

A higher consciousness perspective on the Transgender Agenda; what it is and why it is being rolled out at breakneck speed to socially engineer a gender dysphoria epidemic. Available in print and digital editions.

## When Nothing Else Works: How To Cure Your Lower Back Pain Fast!

The simple method that no doctor will ever tell you about. Requires no drugs, no surgery, and no special equipment. Available in print and digital editions.

# About the Author

S. F. Howe is a psychologist, author and spiritual teacher. Howe began teaching psychology at the university level while a doctoral candidate in clinical psychology, and went on to work in hospitals and clinics for more than 25 years as a psychotherapist, staff psychologist, clinical program consultant and director of chemical dependency and psychiatric programs.

In the midst of graduate studies, a profound spiritual awakening led to a complete reevaluation of the author's life path. Thus began a spiritual journey along the road less traveled, extending far beyond clinical psychology, conventional reality paradigms and both traditional religion and new age spirituality.

While engaged in a unique, ongoing process of discovery, the author enjoys sharing with others an ever-expanding understanding of the true nature of personal reality. This has resulted in Howe's noted books and teachings on the subjects of higher consciousness, conscious health, personal growth and plant intelligence.

Howe's primary intention is to bring an end to suffering by guiding others on a well-worn path to truth and expanded awareness.

Many of those who have experienced Howe's input and presence report emotional and physical healing, life-changing realizations and dramatic personal transformation.

S. F. Howe may be contacted for speaking and teaching engagements. Please direct all inquiries to info@diamondstarpress.com.

# Bonus Gift

As my thanks to you for reading *Vision Board Success: How to Get Everything You Want With Vision Boards!* I would like you to have a free starter library of two bonus ebooks, "The Law of Attraction" and "The Secrets of Success." The information and techniques offered in these ebooks perfectly complement *Vision Board Success.* They will increase your understanding of how to use the power of Vision Boards to achieve your goals, and accelerate your progress toward creating an ideal and fulfilling life.

To receive your free gift, just send an email to info@diamondstarpress.com with proof of purchase and "Send Vision Board Gift" in the subject field, and we will get your bonus ebooks out to you right away. Do it now before you forget!

www.ingramcontent.com/pod-product-compliance
Lightning Source LLC
Chambersburg PA
CBHW061457040426
42450CB00008B/1402